RIVER
Through the Ages

PHILIP STEELE

Illustrated by
ROBERT INGPEN

Troll Associates

Library of Congress Cataloging-in-Publication Data

Steele, Philip
    River through the ages / by Philip Steele, illustrated by Robert
Ingpen.
        p.   cm.
    Summary: Follows human activities around fictitious rivers as
they represent the development of civilization over thousands of
years, from the visits of Stone Age hunters to modern efforts to
stem pollution.
    ISBN 0-8167-2735-X (lib. bdg.)   ISBN 0-8167-2736-8 (pbk.)
    1. Rivers–Juvenile literature.   [1. Rivers.   2. Civilization–
History.]   I. Ingpen, Robert R., ill.   II. Title.
GB1203.8.S83   1993
910'.021693–dc20   91-33279

Published by Troll Associates
© 1994 Eagle Books

Design by James Marks

Printed in the U.S.A.

10 9 8 7 6 5 4 3 2 1

Introduction

Rivers shaped the landscape long before humans appeared on Earth. Sometimes rivers ran swiftly through lush fields. At other times when there were droughts, the riverbeds lay dry and cracked. Fifteen thousand years ago many rivers were frozen glaciers, grinding out deep valleys in an icy landscape. Then they melted as the climate warmed once more.

The rivers provided a home for fish, birds, and mammals. Humans were attracted to rivers for food and water, and they also learned to use them to travel swiftly from one region to another. Riverbanks became a desirable place to build towns and cities.

The rivers in this book do not appear on any maps, because they are imaginary. However, there are many like them in the world.

Contents

The ancient river

For thousands of years the river carried rain and melting snow from the hills. It was fed by mountain streams that tumbled over waterfalls. It was joined by smaller rivers, or tributaries. It wound, or meandered, across a grassy plain. The rushing waters washed away soil and wore down rock. Each spring its waters flooded, leaving behind layers of mud. Finally it broadened, forming an estuary. Sea birds wheeled over sandbanks at low tide.

Stone-Age hunters had visited the estuary for thousands of years. By 6000 B.C., they were making canoes from hollowed-out tree trunks and paddling upstream. They fished, trapped wildfowl, and hunted deer in the forest.

Fish spears were made of antler horn lashed to wood. Resin from plants was used to attach tiny, razor-sharp flints to arrow shafts. Fishhooks were made of bone.

Women and children searched the shallows for shellfish, and cooked fish over the campfire. Boulders were placed in the deeper channels as stepping stones.

Riverside village

By 2000 B.C. there were villages of thatched huts along some riverbanks. Villagers still made weapons of flint and hunted along the valley, and they still trapped eels and fish along the banks. But, they had also learned to till the soil. Barley was growing in the rich, muddy soil left behind by the floods each spring. Sheep and cattle grazed on the valley slopes.

Near one village, a low bridge had been made by placing slabs of stone over boulders.

In peaceful times, traders sailed up the river or rode along the coast on sturdy ponies. As they splashed through the shallows, excited villagers rushed out to meet them. The traders brought pots, necklaces, and knives made of copper.

The river now marked the border of the tribe's territory. Strangers sometimes crossed the river to steal cattle. The village was set on fire several times and villagers died defending their homes.

Children spotted them first: two warriors were creeping through the reeds on the riverbank. The animals were quickly herded into pens. Babies cried as they were snatched up and carried into the huts. The villagers prepared to defend their homes.

The enemy band soon appeared on the opposite bank. Their leaders leapt into the shallows, yelling and brandishing spears. The villagers knew the fight would be fierce.

Roman rule

Celtic settlers along this riverbank were master metalworkers in bronze and iron. When Roman soldiers invaded this settlement, the defeated Celts were set to work.

A large port was built on the estuary. The oak forests were cleared for their timber. Stone was quarried upstream and brought down the river by barge. Houses and shops on both sides of the river were linked by a bridge.

By the year A.D. 200 the region was peaceful and prosperous. Ships brought luxury goods from the Mediterranean and returned there with locally woven woolen cloaks and lead from the inland mines. A tower was built at the mouth of the river with a beacon which guided ships into the harbor. The smoke from the signal fire could be seen for miles. Soldiers kept a lookout for pirates and enemy ships.

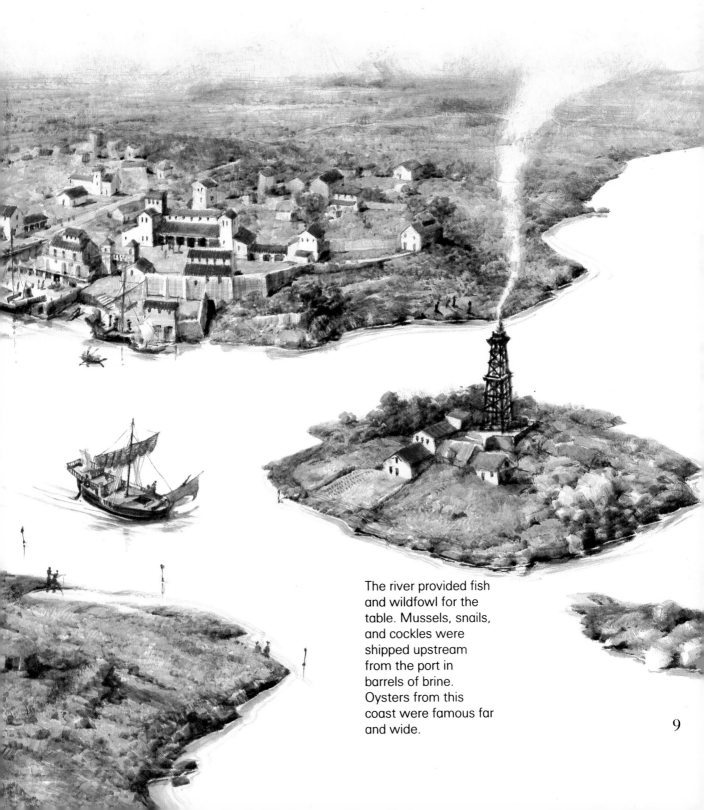

The river provided fish and wildfowl for the table. Mussels, snails, and cockles were shipped upstream from the port in barrels of brine. Oysters from this coast were famous far and wide.

Viking invasion

After 400, the Romans lost control of the province. Soon their ships were no longer moored in the river.

Now the beacon was mostly lit as a warning, because warrior bands often sailed up the river, stealing cattle and raiding stores of grain.

During the later years of Roman rule, Christianity became popular. Many followed this faith after the Romans left, and in 550 a small church was built upstream, where the river descended from the hills. A village grew up around the church.

In 800, Viking warriors from Scandinavia burned the port to the ground. They filled their long, narrow sailing ships with loot and sailed away. In 850 they returned and built a town on the site of the old port. A hundred years later, local people rebelled, and the long ships sailed away forever.

Women and children ran for the woods as the Vikings swarmed ashore. The priest tried to bury the church's valuables, but he and many villagers were killed.

The Middle Ages

The Vikings' descendants, called Normans, built this city on a riverbank in 1080. A stone church was built in 1150. Around it were a dozen houses thatched with reeds. Oxen drank from the river, churning the banks into deep mud.

The water mill ground wheat into flour. The grinding stones were driven by a water wheel. This was turned by water from a channel, or millrace. Ducks swam on the millpond.

A shallow part of the river allowed people on horseback to cross, or ford, the river at this point. Travelers on foot had to call for the ferryman. In 1350 an arched stone bridge was constructed and new houses made of stone were built on the opposite bank.

The villagers depended on the river. It provided fish and fowl for eating, reeds for roofing and basketry, water for thirsty animals, and power for the mill. On hot days children who had been working in the fields dived into its cool waters or skipped stones across the millpond.

13

The river as a road

By 1530, a small city had grown up at the mouth of another river. There was a royal palace and a magnificent cathedral. A bridge, built in 1450, was lined with houses and shops.

The roads were in very poor condition, so members of the royal family and important church officials often traveled by river. Their splendid barges were decorated with flags. Many less important people also rowed up and down the river or traveled as passengers in small boats.

As the city grew, people changed the way they treated the river. They threw rubbish into it. The people in this city no longer fished and swam in the river.

Below the town, where the river broadened into an estuary, the winds blew fresh air from the sea. Here there were large sailing ships at anchor. Some had recently arrived from the Spanish Main, the coast of northern South America. Others were coasters or small boats engaged in trade with the growing towns upstream.

Backwaters and stairs were dirty and foul-smelling. Ladies traveling by river carried bunches of flowers to sweeten the air they breathed.

Draining the wetlands

Many miles away, another river drained a large area of wetland, or fen. For as long as anyone could remember, the marshes had been covered in reeds. It was a lonely place, suitable only for wild ducks and geese.

In 1660, the owner of the land decided to drain the marshes. He persuaded others to put money into the enterprise. After all, this wilderness could be turned into profitable farmland.

An engineer was hired to supervise the work. Vast areas of the Netherlands had already been reclaimed from sea and swamp. This tributary was to be dredged and deepened. A series of channels was to be dug across the fen. The water level of these sluices could be controlled by wooden gates.

Not everyone welcomed the engineering works. Local people relied on the fens for their livelihood, selling

reeds for thatching and catching fish. Some of them broke open the sluice gates at night and flooded the workings. The engineer saw the job through, however. Soon the fens were being turned into fields.

Some local landowners also disliked the changes being made to the fens. They liked to hunt on the marshes and would wait in the reed beds on misty mornings. As the ducks flew by, they were shot down with long-barreled, beautifully decorated guns called "fowling pieces."

A new canal

During the 1770s, a large inland town needed a waterway. Its famous pottery needed to be transported to the coast, so it was decided to dig a canal across the country. This was to be linked to a river, upstream from a great port.

Gangs of workmen came to dig the new canal. They were known as "navigators" or "navvies," and they were a wild group. Their work camps were notorious for fighting. Local people were relieved when the canal was finally completed.

The canal was built over rising ground. In order to keep the course level, locks had to be built. These had huge gates that controlled the water level. Narrow boats entered the lock at one level. The lock gates closed behind them. Water flooded in until the barge reached the upper level. The forward gates were then opened and the barge could continue on its way.

Beside the canal was a towpath. This was a passageway for the horses or mules that hauled the narrow boats along the canal.

Canals like this one were successful. They were used for over a hundred years. But from the 1840s onward, canals had to compete with the new railways and with better roads.

The river freezes

The winter of 1830 was a harsh one. Snow fell in November, and just before Christmas the canal and the upper reaches of the river froze over completely.

The children were excited. They slid on the ice from dawn until dusk. Their parents warned them about thin ice. One boy did fall in, but he was rescued.

Parties traveled by horse-drawn coach. They attached skate blades to their boots and glided across the ice arm in arm. One young man tried to impress the young ladies by skating in circles. He fell flat on his face, and everyone laughed. Many of the visitors had bruised limbs the next day.

Traders set up stalls on the snowy banks and sold hot chestnuts. Pies were sold from the backs of farm carts. The cold weather lasted until the middle of January.

All shipping came to a halt when the river and the canal froze. Many people lost their wages. The poor and elderly suffered in the cold.

New bridges

By 1850, the port at the mouth of the river had grown larger. There were now long docks, where many tall sailing ships were moored. Chests of tea from China were stacked in warehouses, and coal shipped from the north was piled up on the wharves. Where the river passed through the city, high embankments had been built to prevent flooding.

Old bridges had been replaced. An arched stone bridge linked the city center with new, sprawling suburbs on the opposite bank.

The bridges across the river were large and impressive. They were a symbol of prosperous times for the river and its towns.

22

Downstream from the docks, a suspension bridge linked sections of a coastal road. Its deck was supported by huge chains of wrought iron that hung from two high towers. The carriageway was 100 feet (30 meters) above the water line so that tall ships could pass underneath.

The newest bridge was built farther upstream from the center. It was designed to carry the new railway and was made of strong iron girders. The towers for this bridge were built in the middle of the river.

Huge caissons, enclosures made of iron, were lowered into the river and set into the riverbed. The water was then pumped out of the caissons, so that the brick and stone foundations of the towers could be built on the dry riverbed.

In later years, many more bridges were built across the river. From the 1870s they were made of steel, a strengthened form of iron. Metal bridges had to be strong enough to stand up to high winds, flooding, and the river's strong current.

The sprawling city

During the 19th century, the river became increasingly dirty. As the city grew, more and more sewage was piped into the river. Factories spewed industrial waste into the river, too. For centuries salmon had swum upstream to their breeding grounds. Now they had disappeared altogether.

In the 1880s, a new sewage system was built. Drinking water was piped down from the mountains, where a lake was enlarged to make a reservoir and a clean water supply. Public health began to improve.

By 1900, two tunnels were built under the river to carry an underground railroad.

Large steamships now anchored at the docks, although there were still a few tall sailing ships and barges. Some people feared that mud, or silt, would block the river mouth. Steam dredgers deepened the channels leading to the port so that even the larger ships could dock safely.

Buoys marked the navigation channels. Launches took pilots out to incoming vessels, and these officers guided the captains of the ships to their moorings.

In 1900, the docks and backwaters were not fashionable. Here the factories backed onto banks of mud. Poor people turned over discarded odds and ends in search of valuables.

The hydroelectric system

High in the mountains, the upper reaches of the river had changed little since prehistoric times. Springs and waterfalls fed sparkling streams. Walkers still crossed brooks over ancient stepping stones.

However, in 1950 a dam was built across the mountain valley. A huge concrete barrier held back the river water. The force of the water was then used to drive the blades of turbines in a power station. The whirling machines generated electricity. Tall steel towers were built in the valley to carry power lines to the city.

As the water level rose behind the dam, whole villages had to be moved. Shepherds' huts and old churches disappeared beneath the new lake. Wildlife had to be rescued. Many people protested against the loss of the valley and its villages.

Today, the lake is used for boating and water-skiing in summer. New plants have grown on the banks, and in the winter gulls gather here in the thousands.

This hydroelectric system harnessed the force of water to make electricity. It proved to be a clean and safe way of generating power. However, building the dam was costly, and the engineers had to solve many problems before the dam could operate.

The present

The city at the mouth of the river became an international business center. The docks closed when a new port for container ships opened to the east, and in 1990 the old wharves were turned into a yacht marina.

The river was still busy. There were sightseeing launches, river-police vessels, barges, and dredgers. A hydrofoil ferry skimmed over the water at great speed. The canal, which had been unused for many years, also reopened in 1990 as a tourist attraction.

Low-lying parts of the city were now protected against flooding by a levee. When storms or unusually high tides threatened, huge steel gates were raised from the riverbed to halt the surge.

Every now and then the river
yielded up secrets of its distant past.
When the flood barrier was being
built, workmen uncovered the remains
of a Viking long ship in the mud of the
river.

The view from the top of the skyscraper
offered an aerial view of the river as it
curved through the city. Its broad bends
sparkled in the spring sunshine.

Fish had begun to return to the river,
for its waters were now cleaner.
Factory waste and sewage disposal
were more strictly controlled.

29

The future

Ever since the Stone Age, people have used the river for power, transportation, drinking water, and fishing. They have blocked it with dams and bridges. They have drained its marshes and changed its course. Unfortunately, some people even continue to pollute it. But at last more people are beginning to understand that pollution must stop.

For thousands of years, the endlessly flowing river has carried water from the mountains to the sea. In the future, more and more of us will be doing our best to protect the river and preserve it for future generations.

The river will always be a source of pleasure to children for swimming and boating. Parts of the riverside will be preserved for wildlife. If this is done with care, the number of birds nesting and living by the river will increase.

Index